Imagining the Future

HOUSES

of the PAST, PRESENT, and FUTURE

Linda Bozzo

Bailey Books
an imprint of
Enslow Publishers, Inc.
40 Industrial Road
Box 398
Berkeley Heights, NJ 07922
USA
http://www.enslow.com

Bailey Books, an imprint of Enslow Publishers, Inc.

Library of Congress Cataloging-in-Publication Data

Bozzo, Linda.
 Houses of the past, present, and future / Linda Bozzo.
 p. cm. — (Imagining the future)
 Includes bibliographical references and index.
 Summary: "Read about the history, present, and imagine the future of things in our
   houses, such as the television, dishwasher, bathroom, refrigerator, vacuum cleaner,
   washing machine, milk and butter, and the sewing machine"—Provided by publisher.
 ISBN 978-0-7660-3433-4 (alk. paper)
 1. Dwellings—United States—History—Juvenile literature. 2. Dwellings—Technological
   innovations—United States—Juvenile literature. 3. Home economics—United States—
   History—Juvenile literature. I. Title.
 TX301.B623 2011
 643'.1—dc22   2010002350

Printed in the United States of America
052010 Lake Book Manufacturing, Inc., Melrose Park, IL

10 9 8 7 6 5 4 3 2 1

Illustration Credits: Classic Stock, p. 12 (top); Getty Images News/Getty Images, pp. 14 (bottom),
22 (bottom); Index Stock Imagery/Photolibrary, p. 6 (top); ©iStockphoto.com/Andrea Gingerich,
p. 4; ©iStockphoto.com/Justin Horrocks, p. 5; Tom LaBaff, pp. 1, 7, 9, 11, 13, 15, 17, 19, 21; Library
of Congress, pp. 8 (top), 18 (top), 20 (top); OJO Images/Photolibrary, p. 6 (bottom); Photos.com,
p. 12 (bottom); Shutterstock.com, pp. 3, 8 (bottom), 10 (bottom), 16 (bottom), 18 (bottom), 20
(bottom); Sparrnestad Photo/Peike Reintes, p. 14 (top); © Wisconsin Histocial Society/courtesy
Everett Collection, pp. 2, 10 (top), 16 (top), 22 (top).

Cover Illustrations: front cover—Tom LaBaff; back cover—©iStockphoto.com/Andrea
Gingerich (inset top left); ©iStockphoto.com/Justin Horrocks (inset top right).

CONTENTS

The History of Houses

Yesterday

Your house or home is where you live. Homes have changed over the years. They have become larger and have more rooms.

Today

Many new appliances appeared in homes in the 1900s. Did you know that many years ago, not every home had a bathtub or an indoor toilet?

Tomorrow

Can you imagine what the houses of the **future** will be like?

1. Television

Yesterday

Televisions used to look like this. The first television shows were in black and white.

Today

Now televisions look like this. Shows are now in color.

What if one day you could watch television shows in **3-D** without 3-D glasses? What shows would you like to watch in 3-D?

2. Dishwasher

Yesterday

In the past, dishes could only be washed by hand.

Today

Today, machines called dishwashers are in many homes.

What if there were a new way to clean dishes? You put dishes in the cupboard and close the door. Beams of light zap the dishes clean. Just think of how much water you could save. There would be no need to put away the dishes. They are in the cupboard, ready to use again.

3. Bathroom

Yesterday

At one time there were no toilets inside the house. People used an **outhouse**.

Today

Today, homes have toilets in their bathrooms. They have sinks and bathtubs or showers.

Many years from now, what do you think bathrooms will look like? What if bathtubs could make you super clean? You would not have to take another bath for weeks!

4. Refrigerator

People once used iceboxes like this one to keep their food cool.

Today

Today, refrigerators store cold food. One part is so cold that it can freeze food.

12

What if your refrigerator could talk? It might tell you what food is inside. What else might it say? What if it could print out a shopping list for your mother?

5. Vacuum Cleaner

Yesterday

Long ago, people cleaned rugs by hitting them with rug beaters to knock off the dirt and dust.

Today

Today, there are **robot vacuums**. They clean even when you are not home.

What do you think the vacuums of tomorrow might look like? Imagine having a vacuum you could ride. That would make cleaning your room more fun!

6. Washing Machine

Yesterday

People used to wash clothes in a washtub.

Today

Today, washing machines clean dirt from clothes.

What if one machine could wash and dry your clothes too? It might even fold them. The washing machines of tomorrow would never lose socks.

7. Groceries

Yesterday

Long ago, milkmen brought milk to people's houses in glass bottles. People made their own butter.

Today

Today, we buy milk, butter, and other food at the grocery store.

What if you never had to go to the grocery store again? Your food could travel through tubes right into your home. Cold food would go right to your refrigerator. No more carrying or unpacking food from bags.

8. Clothes

Yesterday

The sewing machine was one of the first machines found in homes. People once sewed their clothes on machines that looked like this.

Today

Today, most people buy their clothes at stores instead of sewing them.

What if you could draw clothes on a computer? You pick the colors. You tell it your size. The computer does the sewing. In just minutes, out come your new clothes!

The world we live in is always changing. No one really knows what will happen in the future. We can only imagine!

WORDS TO KNOW

3-D—Three-dimensional things have length, width, and depth.

appliances—Machines found in homes.

future—The time after today.

outhouse—A small building with a type of toilet inside.

robot—A machine that does work on its own.

vacuum (VACK-yum)—A cleaning machine that picks up dirt.

Learn More

Books

Nelson, Robin. *Home Then and Now*. Minneapolis: Lerner Publications, 2003.

Shoulders, Michael. *The ABC Book of American Homes*. Watertown, Mass.: Charlesbridge, 2008.

Yates, Vicki. *Life at Home*. Chicago: Heinemann Library, 2008.

Web Sites

PBS: Technology at Home: You Try It
<http://www.pbs.org/wgbh/aso/tryit/tech>

PBS: The 1900 House
<http://www.pbs.org/wnet/1900house>

INDEX